REMEMBER ANYTHING 10X MORE EFFECTIVELY

Discover How to Train your Mind with quick memory improvement techniques. Memorize names and remember things better (tips and tricks guidebook)

Steve Lowndes & Ian Leil

Legal Notice:

This book is copyright protected. This book is only for personal use. You cannot amend, distribute, sell, use, quote or paraphrase any part, or the content within this book, without the consent of the author or publisher.

Disclaimer Notice:

Please note the information contained within this document is for educational and entertainment purposes only. All effort has been executed to present accurate, up to date, and reliable, complete information. No warranties of any kind are declared or implied. Readers acknowledge that the author is not engaging in the rendering of legal, financial, medical or professional advice. The content within this book has been derived from various sources. Please consult a licensed professional before attempting any techniques outlined in this book.

By reading this document, the reader agrees that under no circumstances is the author responsible for any losses, direct or indirect, which are incurred as a result of the use of the information contained within this document, including, but not limited to, —

errors, omissions, or inaccuracies.

TABLE OF CONTENTS

INTRODUCTION

How can you achieve a better memory and improve your ability to quickly recall information?

During the course of our lives we all happen to live sudden moments of empty mindedness during which we feel absent minded or as if we are forgetting something.

When this happens too often, it's usually a sign of bad memory and if you are a perfectionist like myself, you will want to fix this.

So, what can you immediately do to boost your memory?

Worry not, this is what this book is all about and before we dig deeper into its content, here's a little piece of advice for you: if you can - you should take notes. This is how you will jumpstart your memory improvement.

Have you ever walked into a room and suddenly forgot why you are there? Have you ever gone to the supermarket to buy milk and came back with two bags full of all sorts of groceries but the milk? Have you ever gotten past a few pages of a book and suddenly realized you could not remember a single word you just read?

Then this book is just what you need: make sure to pay close attention to it and give it your full focus.

There is one phrase we all hate using when we forget something. Whether it's related to your job or to your personal life, saying those two terrible words "I FORGOT", causes nothing but disappointment.

" I Forgot to bring it to the meeting "

" I Forgot to do it "

" I Forgot I put that there "

" I Forgot what you told me earlier "

" I Forgot about that meeting "

" I Forgot that person's name "

These are all phrases that besides the awkwardness they cause, can also cost you a fortune.

For instance, how are you going to even express any interest or talk to someone openly if you can't even remember their name? If you're growing a business, how can you show that you care about other people and help them with their life or their finances if you don't remember their names, and then, how can you grow your network efficiently if you are unable to even simply remember their names? It will give people the impression that you don't care about them, even if you truly do.

In this book you will discover the three very effective methods to quickly boost your memory and improve your ability to recall automatically information..

Just to give you an example: How comes the best memory experts do live presentations on stages and are able to memorize the name of every single person in the room or hundreds of words and numbers in sequence in the blink of an eye?

They don't just do it to impress the audience. This is a way to express what is truly possible by training your mind and improving your memory. As a matter of fact, you can do the exact same thing too, regardless of your age, emotional or financial situation. Your background doesn't matter, your personality does not matter and nor does your career.

A common belief is that your capability of learning something or even your intelligence and memory are somehow fixed and cannot be developed or changed unless you were born with certain talents.

This is not true, sure some people might have slight advantages but your brain is like a white canvas waiting for you to paint on it. You can create new patterns all the time.

As a matter of fact we have recently discovered a lot more about the human brain than in the past twenty years and new ways to train it and improve its performance have been developed, no matter your age.

In reality there's no such thing as good and bad memory: there's only trained and untrained memory.

Here's an example: a school is generally a good place to learn. You can learn a lot of things about maths, history, science, literature and many other subjects.

But a very very small number of classes actually teach you " How to learn " and how to think in different ways, how to solve problems, how to be creative, how to stay focused, concentrated, how to be productive and so on.

They don't teach you how to train your brain and improve your memory in school.

I already wrote a book about how you can learn anything 10 times faster, check it out on Amazon or Audible if you're interested as joining together my teachings from both books will quite literally upgrade you to a better version of yourself in no time.

These subjects were problematic to me, in fact I always had problem with focus and procrastinations and as you can tell, by now I've become nearly obsessed with finding new ways to improve myself, how can I improve my focus and concentration? How can i improve my brain?

How could I improve my memory in order for it to work better?

Here's one thing I want you to remember: researcher state that one third of our brain (and so, our memory) is predetermined by biology and genetics. It is only one third.

What about the others two thirds ? What this means is that the others two thirds are subjects to our control. And by our control, I mean our total control.

We just don't really know that.

As a matter of fact you don't want to learn new skills or something new, or go to an important seminar or read a book or in general do things that are important to you, without being able to retain them.

If you don't retain your important experiences or achievements, is it like they never happened to you, right?

Let's go straight to the point and discover together the 3 key methods to improve your memory quickly and effectively.

CHAPTER 1:
THE R.A.P. METHOD

The first thing I want you to remember is the word RAP R.A.P. Yeah, like the music genre, RAP, all right? It may sound ironic or like I'm joking, but I'm actually very serious, so whether you like that music genre or not, it doesn't matter, you will agree that it's still quite an easy word to remember, right?

R. A. P.

What do these letters stand for?

For a brief moment, just focus on the word itself and memorize it. I want you to give importance to this word: RAP

Repeat after me, RAP, R A P.

Are you ready? Perfect, let's keep going, I'll explain to you this incredible method that will instantly boost your memory.

We will start off by checking what each letter represents.

CHAPTER 2:
THE LETTER R

As i said before, keep it mind the word RAP.

R is the first letter.

Before i tell you what the R means, i want to ask a question to you :

Let's implement this to " Remember people's Names "

It may sound funny but this is like a sport so we want to get good at it.

If you want to improve your memory as well as remember names, you have to become good at it . This principle can be applied to many things.

Maybe you would like to become a better businessman, or a better musician, or improve your learning and reading skills, you have to train and become good at it.

Do you Remember what i said initially ? There is no good or bad memory. There is only trained and untrained memory.

So let's apply this concept to memory and take remembering names as an example.

Most people, when they get to know another person, right after they've introduced themselves by saying their name, suddenly forget the name they were told.

How many times has this happened to you?

I bet at least once. When it starts happening all the time, then you have a problem to solve. If every time we meet a new person, we can't remember the name right afterwards and this is a standard pattern, we will have to train.

Literally, you just met a person, they told you their name and a few seconds later *POOF* it just disappears from your head. That memory lasted barely throughout the handshake.

For now, don't stress it too much, it happens to the best of us and it's extremely common.

But what if there's a way to get out of that awkward situation?

This is called the six second syndrome. And to overcome it, there is a procedure:

You have to do something with that name within the first six seconds after hearing it to avoid its disappearance.

Here's an example:

Let's assume that you usually have trouble remembering someone's name.

Now, let's assume that there is a bag full of moneys, 200.000 $.

Now, you are going to earn those 200.000 $ if you can remember the name of the first next person you meet without having to hear it a second time.

Do you think you are going to remember that person's name in this case?

I bet you will, of course you are.

And that is because you have a purpose and you are motivated.

So the R in RAP stands for REASON.

For instance, it is like you always had issues remembering names before, and now you suddenly become an expert in people's names.

And it is because you are MOTIVATED. There is a REASON why you have to do it.

Again, remember that the R in RAP stands for REASON, and it has nothing to do with your capability to stay motivated in general during your day.

Since I want you to reach higher standards and have a better memory, keep in mind that this next segment doesn't really have anything to do with your ability to remember names, it's strictly related just to your general memory improvement. Here's a small challenge:

How can you improve your motivation in order to better your memory?

It is actually pretty simple: you have to ask yourself " Why? " all the time.

Let's examine the world Why. So simple yet so complex, it leads to further questions:

What is my reason why?

What's in it for me?

Why should i do that?

What you should ask yourself when you meet someone for the first time, in order to improve your memory is:

Why do I want to remember this?

This applies to pretty much any situation and every other subject:

Why do I want to remember this language?

Why do I want to remember what this person says?

Why do I want to remember this number?

As a matter of fact, if you can't come up with a reason to remember one specific thing, then you most likely won't remember it or you will forget it soon enough.

But if you are moved by a reason, you will automatically get much better results.

The simple trick to jumpstart your motivation is to ask yourself the question " Why do i want to remember this? "

So, whether it's remembering a person's name, or doing something for yourself or learning something new, always check your REASON to do it.

The first and most important thing that truly matters at the start of your journey is your REASON.

CHAPTER 3:
THE LETTER A

With the second method to quickly improve your memory, we are going to unzip the meaning of the letter A.

So, the A in RAP stands for ATTENTION.

I will repeat it again and I invite you to do the same with me.

The A in RAP stands for ATTENTION.

ATTENTION.

Pretty much as i said at the beginning of this book, the most common thought people have is "Oh I have terrible memory".

They will justify this by thinking that it's due to their age or genetics or anything else related to their current situation and how they have been educated.

Here's the thing:

When you are fighting in favor of your own limitations, the only result you will achieve is to keep them. If you justify your limitations you will get nowhere.

Error is only human, but to persist in it, is diabolical!

I will say this again : When you are fighting in favor of your own limitations, the only result you will achieve is to keep them.

What you need to do immediately is to cease negatively talking yourself down. Eliminate the negative thoughts.

It's a harmful system which activates when you are in trouble and that makes you think negatively of yourself in order to justify your faults or not putting effort into something.

And the worst part is that this does nothing but hurt yourself.

We can call this as auto-negative self talk.

What you want to do is at least to diminish it, or better, again, get rid of it.

People who complain about their memory are just part of a bigger category who likes to blame their faults on external factors.

I know this kind of people well, I was one of those.

The thing is that if you are not the first one believing that you can achieve better results, then you most likely won't.

Improving your memory lies in your ability to observate. In your attention.

It is all related to your attention.

Take for example the biggest businessmen and leaders in various sectors.

Successful people are constantly trying to improve themselves, reading books, becoming educated and learning new things.

Surprisingly, they all have one thing in common:

They have a very good memory.

Why they have good memory?

It is because they chose to care about it. They care about things and they care about remembering things they care about.

I know that sounded like a tongue twister but it makes perfect sense.

For instance, after a speech at an event and telling a story, they ask questions to their audience to check if they were paying attention to what they were saying.

Because in the end ATTENTION is all that matters.

You will notice this on yourself too when you participate to an event. Some people will have an undivided attention, or, as you look over your shoulder, you will notice some others are distracted like you are at that very moment.

You don't distract yourself just on the outside by splitting your attention between several things that are happening around you, you distract yourself on the inside too by getting lost in your own thoughts and talking to yourself instead of paying attention to a conversation or to this very same audiobook.

What you may call listening is not really listening. That is just waiting for your turn to participate.

Waiting for your turn to speak. Waiting for your turn to change what do you want to change.

You find yourself waiting to respond to something and that is not paying attention.

So in order to boost your memory, not only your reason

to remember things is important, but also your attention to it.

What successful people have, besides often having good communication skills, charisma and especially in this case a good memory, also comes from having an active presence.

And it is not just a matter of having a good presence per se, but of having a good presence with people, and therefore, a good presence for the things that matter.

This is something you can do too, let's take a step back to remembering names, you not only want to have a reason to remember their name, but you also want to be THERE with them, you want people to KNOW that you are actively there paying ATTENTION.

This is one simple way to impress people because you will convey to them that you care.

Also, you will impress yourself, because all of a sudden you will think of why you care about them, why you care about the things that matter to you.

If you think about the verb "to listen", what other words come to your mind?

In my case, SILENCE.

The word Silence.

My number 1 advice to improve your attention is to listen. To listen in silence. Be silent and observe.

Be present and silent, and you will remember that name, you will remember that thing they just said.

CHAPTER 4:
THE LETTER P

So we've come to the last letter of the word RAP, the P.

The P in RAP stands for Practice.

How do you remember things if you don't put them into practice?

How do you learn new things if you don't learn.

These are the procedures you will need to follow. You have to practice the things you learn. Like what you've learned so far in this book.

If you want to improve your memory, you have to start putting your newly learned knowledge into practice.

You have to stick to procedures that improve your memory.

Use what you learned in this book, not one time, not ten times, but as many times as possible, like, every time. And trust me, you will enjoy your super memory boost.

CONCLUSION

Improving our ability to memorize and understand others is an incredibly serious step we all need to make in order to improve ourselves and to reach our objectives.

Remember, when you are trying to build a skill, you're trying to rewire your brain, create new neural pathways.

This takes a lot of willpower.

Be patient and keep trying. The results will come in no time bringing nothing but positive responses from the people around you.

Improving your technique using the methods I illustrated in this book will do wonders.

Get back in action and let me know how it goes.

Try out these tricks and improve!

Best of luck see you in the next book.

ACKNOWLEDGEMENTS

The purpose of our books is to make your life better by improving the very fundamental way you learn new things and clear your confusion and bad habits.

We want to thank you for taking action by reading this book and we hope that you keep on using these simple and efficient methods in order to reach your goal. If you found this helpful, we hope that you can spread the word to everyone around you who struggles with the same problems in order to help them.

We also want to thank all of the members of our publishing team for making this possible.

A special thanks goes also to all of the researchers who study this matter every day at the cost of their own sleep to help us improve our life.

Thank you all.

www.ingramcontent.com/pod-product-compliance
Lightning Source LLC
Chambersburg PA
CBHW072131150726
47999CB00005B/2237